GENOCIDE IN MODERN TIMES™

GENOCIDE IN RWANDA

Frank Spalding

ROSEN
PUBLISHING®

New York

Published in 2009 by The Rosen Publishing Group, Inc.
29 East 21st Street, New York, NY 10010

Library of Congress Cataloging-in-Publication Data

Spalding, Frank.
Genocide in Rwanda / Frank Spalding. — 1st ed.
    p. cm.—(Genocide in modern times)
Includes bibliographical references and index.
ISBN-13: 978-1-4042-1823-9 (library binding)
1. Genocide—Rwanda—History—20th century—Juvenile literature.
2. Rwanda—History—Civil War, 1994—Juvenile literature. 3. Rwanda—Ethnic relations—History—20th century—Juvenile literature. I. Title.
DT450.435.S68 2008
967.57104'31—dc22
                                                        2007053032

Manufactured in the United States of America

On the cover: Background: Children play on a tree in a camp in southern Rwanda where more than eight thousand Tutsi refugees gathered under the protection of French soldiers. Foreground: Survivors of the 1994 genocide carry the coffins of the victims in Kigali, Rwanda.

CONTENTS

INTRODUCTION

World War II (1939–1945) was the most destructive armed conflict in the twentieth century. Many of the world's nations chose sides, joining either the Allied powers, which included countries such as Britain, Canada, and the United States, or the Axis powers, which included Germany, Italy, and Japan. Eventually, the Allies emerged victorious, but not before the war had claimed the lives of more than seventy million people.

One of the most significant tragedies to come to light at the end of the war was Nazi Germany's systematic attempt to exterminate certain groups of people, like the handicapped, homosexuals, and political enemies. It also included ethnic groups such as the Roma and Jews. The Jews were particularly targeted, with approximately six million of them murdered by the time the war drew to a close.

The Nazis went about the killing methodically. They moved people into

The Rwandan genocide occurred over one hundred days in 1994. During that time, unimaginable horrors occurred. Here, the skull of a person murdered in the genocide lies near human remains.

concentration camps, where they were forced into hard labor. Many starved to death or succumbed to disease; others were executed. The organized murder of a specific group of people is known as genocide, a word invented in 1944 to describe atrocities such as those committed by the Nazis.

The nations of the world vowed that the horrors of World War II would never again be repeated. In an attempt to prevent future worldwide conflict, it was determined that an international organization should be established to further diplomacy and interaction between nations. So, in 1945, the United Nations (UN) was founded. Today, nearly two hundred countries—almost every sovereign nation on Earth—are UN member states.

The internationally accepted legal definition of genocide is found in the United Nations' Convention on the Prevention and Punishment of the Crime of Genocide, which was first drafted on December 11, 1946, and took effect in 1951. It defined genocide as: "Acts committed with intent to destroy, in whole or in part, a national, ethnical, racial, or religious group."

Unfortunately, the international community's efforts have not actually ended genocide. Several genocides have occurred since World War II. In the small nation of Rwanda, located in central Africa, a horrific genocide occurred from April 6, 1994, until the middle of July of that same year. The genocide only lasted one hundred days, but by the time it ended, nearly a million people had been murdered. Most were killed with clubs or machetes. Many were killed by people they knew, even sometimes their neighbors.

The killing was quick and ruthless, conducted in front of a small, virtually powerless UN peacekeeping force. Although politicians around the world knew what was happening in Rwanda, they didn't want to get involved or intervene. By the time they finally did, it was too late for the hundreds of thousands of innocent men, women, and children who had been killed.

1

A Modern History of Rwanda

The small, landlocked nation of Rwanda comprises about 10,000 square miles (25,900 square kilometers). It is approximately the same size as the state of Massachusetts. Located in the middle of the continent, Rwanda is bordered by four countries: Burundi, the Democratic Republic of the Congo (formerly known as Zaire), Tanzania, and Uganda. Nearly ten million people live in Rwanda, making it the most densely populated nation in Africa. The nation's capital, Kigali, is home to nearly one million people. The country is very poor; most Rwandans rely on subsistence agriculture to survive. The economy is bolstered by exports of tea and coffee.

RWANDANS

The peoples that settled Rwanda thousands of years ago farmed and raised cattle. Over time, a sort of aristocracy of powerful people arose. These people eventually became known as the Tutsi, a word that was originally used to refer to someone who owns a lot of cattle. Everyone who was not a Tutsi became a Hutu.

Generally, the Tutsi tended to have lighter complexions and be tall and slender, while the Hutu tended to have darker complexions and be stockier. But the supposed differences in ethnicity or

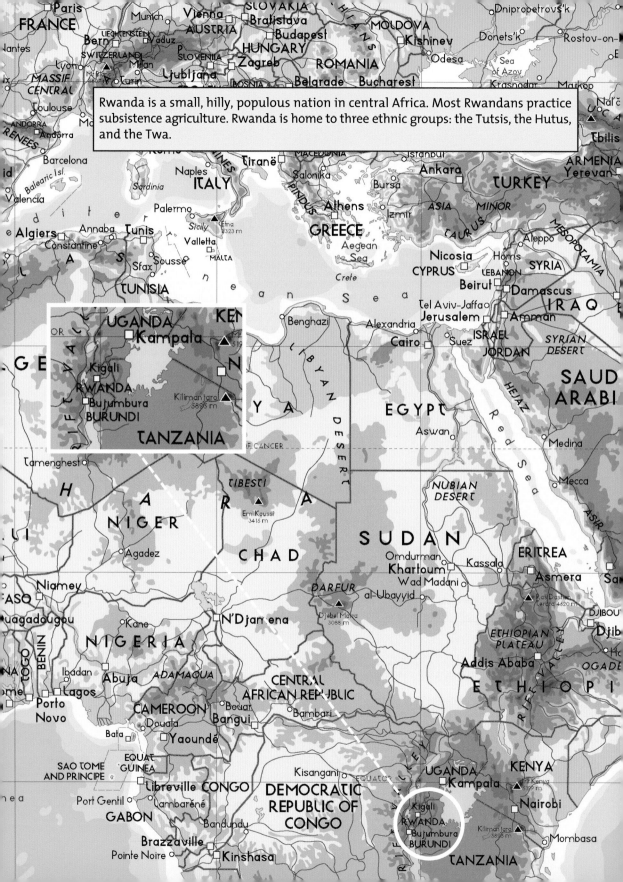

Rwanda is a small, hilly, populous nation in central Africa. Most Rwandans practice subsistence agriculture. Rwanda is home to three ethnic groups: the Tutsis, the Hutus, and the Twa.

appearance between Hutu and Tutsi was, for all intents and purposes, eliminated by intermarriage between the two groups.

There were many more Hutu than Tutsi in Rwanda. The population of Rwanda was about 90 percent Hutu and 10 percent Tutsi. A third group of people, the Twa, who were hunter-gatherer pygmies, made up less than 1 percent of the population. All Rwandans shared the same religion and partook of the same culture. In the past, Rwanda was a monarchy ruled by a king. Even today, though horribly and violently divided, all Rwandans speak the language Kinyarwanda, and many also speak Swahili. French and English are spoken by some, too.

Traditionally, Rwandan Hutus practiced subsistence agriculture to survive. The Tutsis, however, typically raised cattle—which was a much more lucrative occupation. Despite sharing the same culture, a rift grew between the two populations.

UNDER FOREIGN RULE

Ultimately, Rwanda's future would be shaped by European colonialism. Colonialism is the practice of a powerful nation extending its reach by dominating another nation or people. Beginning in 1885, European colonial powers established control over the majority of African nations. When the colonial powers divided up control of the continent, borders were established that typically ignored the existing divisions between different African regions, ethnic groups, and kingdoms.

German colonists arrived in Rwanda in the late nineteenth century. But after Germany's defeat in World War I (1914–1918), it lost control

of Rwanda, which then fell under Belgian control. Belgians altered Rwanda's government by placing Tutsis—and only Tutsis—in positions of power. The Belgians believed that Tutsis had more "Caucasian" features than Hutus and were therefore more fit to rule. Blatantly racist beliefs such as these were not uncommon in Europe at the time.

European colonization had disastrous effects for Africa. Dr. Heinrich Albert Schnee *(left)* and Paul von Lettow-Vorbeck *(right)*, photographed here in 1919, administered a section of Africa colonized by the Germans. This territory, known as German East Africa, encompassed several present-day countries, including Rwanda.

First, however, the Belgians had to determine exactly who was a Hutu and who was a Tutsi. This was a difficult proposition at best. The boundary between the two groups of Rwandans was not fixed: Hutus could become Tutsis and vice versa. The Belgians required every Rwandan to register him- or herself as a Hutu, Tutsi, or Twa. This now made it nearly impossible for a Hutu to become a Tutsi, or vice versa. The population was, quite literally, divided. Beginning in 1933, the Belgians issued ethnic identity cards that everyone was required to carry. Later on, ethnic identity cards would prove to have disastrous consequences for a large portion of the Rwandan population.

A RIFT IN THE POPULATION

The Belgians used Tutsis to help them run the country. In return, Tutsis were granted distinct advantages. They received better educations than Hutus and were largely exempt from the kind of manual labor that was the Hutus' lot in life under Belgian rule. In fact, Tutsis were used by the colonists to oversee and manage Hutus engaged in forced labor.

The Hutus' work was so fatiguing that many of them, exhausted by a day of backbreaking work, were too tired to tend their crops. This resulted in massive famines. Eventually, some Rwandans fled to other countries, hoping they would be able to make a better living abroad.

Over the years, the Hutu began to resent the special status granted to the Tutsi. Many began to view the Tutsi in the same way that they saw the colonists: as oppressors.

INDEPENDENCE

By the middle of the twentieth century, a continent-wide movement had begun for African independence. This movement gained popularity in Rwanda, especially among the Hutu. They were tired of being second-class citizens within their own country.

Rwanda was governed by a monarchy until 1961. At that time, King Kigeli V Ndahindurwa sat on the Rwandan throne. He was subsequently forced to live in exile.

In 1959, an uprising that would become known as the Hutu Revolution began. The Hutu wanted to gain greater control over Rwanda. Violence broke out, and hundreds of people lost their lives before peace was restored. The fighting was only a precursor to major changes that would occur. In an effort to quell further conflict, the Belgians replaced a number of Tutsi administrators with Hutus. Then, in 1961, Rwandans voted to abolish their monarchy.

Tutsi rebels mounted a failed invasion of Kigali in 1963. They had a force of several hundred but were defeated before they could even reach Kigali. The Hutu retaliation against Tutsi civilians was quick and brutal. Between the end of December 1962 and early in January 1963, thousands of Tutsis were killed. Men, women, children—anyone who was carrying a Tutsi identity card were targeted. More than two hundred thousand Tutsis fled the country, joining the swelling ranks of Tutsi Rwandan exiles.

A DISPLACED POPULATION

During the Hutu Revolution, approximately ten thousand Tutsis fled the country to live a life of exile. However, they did not forget where they came from and wanted to return. A good portion of these Tutsi exiles stuck together and formed a fighting force. They began launching periodic attacks on Rwanda's Hutu leadership. However, the Tutsi forces in exile were not strong enough to regain control of the government. Their attacks were sometimes used by Hutu "hard-liners," or those Hutus with extreme political beliefs, to turn public sentiment against the Tutsi.

In 1967, eight years after the Hutu Revolution had begun, three hundred thousand more Tutsis were forced into exile. For the time being, exiled Tutsis stopped launching attacks. Within Rwanda, extremists killed twenty thousand Tutsis simply for being Tutsi. Rwanda's Tutsi minority began facing discrimination in areas such as employment.

Throughout all of these political changes, the rigid ethnic classification established by the Belgians persisted. Rwandans knew if their friends and neighbors were Hutu or Tutsi. Tutsis who did not leave Rwanda sometimes figured out ways to have their ethnicity reassigned to become Hutu. By 1991, the Tutsi population was less than half of what it was prior to the Hutu Revolution.

2

The Path to Genocide

In 1973, the man who was to control Rwanda for the next twenty years took power. His name was Juvénal Habyarimana, the general of the Rwandan army. Habyarimana had a vision for Rwanda, which he implemented by forming a political party called the National Revolutionary Movement for Development (MRND). This would soon become Rwanda's only political party.

A NEW LEADER

After reinventing the nation as a one-party state, Habyarimana went about consolidating his power. Since there was no party opposing him, he, in effect, had the support of the entire country's population. Under Habyarimana, the people of Rwanda were forced to participate in manual labor projects designed to maintain Rwanda's roads and land. Improvement of Rwanda's public infrastructure attracted foreign investment, giving the country's economy a boost.

Among his supporters, Habyarimana especially enjoyed strong support from Rwanda's army and police forces. Rwanda had an army known as the Forces Armeés Rwanda (FAR), which included a police force. The police force was known as the Gendarmerie.

Juvénal Habyarimana was the president of Rwanda from 1973 until 1994, when he was killed by unknown assailants. After Habyarimana's death, the tensions that had been simmering in Rwanda exploded into all-out violence.

In addition to this, Habyarimana had a special elite force that was directly under his command, known as the Presidential Guard. Habyarimana's Presidential Guard had upwards of a thousand members. All three of these groups, and their loyalty to their president, would play a key role in the genocide to come.

EXILES

Once Habyarimana became president, organized attacks against Tutsis were effectively brought to an end, although discrimination against them continued. This relative peace didn't mean that Tutsis living abroad were welcomed home, however. Citing Rwanda's chronic overpopulation problem, Habyarimana refused to allow any Tutsi exiles to return to Rwanda. In fact, he even forbade the friends and family members of the exiles from visiting them in the countries where they were living.

The exiles survived as best they could as refugees. In Uganda, for instance, thousands of exiled Tutsis were welcomed into the Ugandan army, where they distinguished themselves as soldiers. Utilizing the training they'd received, they would eventually form their own highly disciplined military organization called the Rwandan Patriotic Front (RPF).

Famine made Rwanda dependent on international aid. Without this aid, people would have starved. This woman helps distribute food in 1990.

ECONOMIC WOES

It seemed that conditions in Rwanda were getting better. True equality had not yet been achieved between the Hutu and Tutsi, and overpopulation was still a problem, but the economy was improving. Foreign investors were eager to put their money into Rwanda. Its main exports, tea and coffee, were selling well.

Things changed dramatically in 1986, when the value of tea and coffee dropped drastically. Suddenly, Rwanda's main exports were no longer very profitable. These economic problems affected the entire population, Hutu and Tutsi alike. Soon, many people were struggling to survive—and the president was losing support.

More than half of Rwanda's income was now provided by foreign aid. Widespread corruption swept the country, as various political and business figures scrambled for economic control. At the same time, in response to international pressure, Habyarimana reluctantly loosened his autocratic control over Rwanda. For the first time in years, opposition parties were allowed to have a token public voice. The Habyarimana regime was not eager to relinquish power, and democracy did not suddenly flourish in Rwanda. Repression against those who dared oppose the government continued.

Habyarimana could not afford to become unpopular among Rwandan Hutus. They were his core supporters. He was also wary of the threat presented by the quarter million Tutsi exiles living just beyond the Rwandan border.

SPREADING HATE

In October 1990, the first RPF invasion of Rwanda took place. Several hundred RPF Tutsis attacked Rwanda but were held off by the army. France and Belgium, longtime supporters of the Habyarimana government, sent troops and weapons to assist in the fight against the RPF.

The RPF would play a key role in bringing the genocide to an end. Here, two RPF soldiers are photographed in 1993, as they make their way to Kigali.

The Habyarimana regime knew it could control the people of Rwanda by blaming the country's problems on a common enemy: the RPF. Extremist factions within the regime began spreading negative propaganda about Tutsis. For instance, they began funding an anti-Tutsi newspaper. This paper published articles on how the Tutsi, as an ethnic group, were allegedly dangerous. It also published the names of Rwandans who were supposedly criminal collaborators with the RPF. Many people were listed who had nothing at all to do with the RPF—their names may have appeared on the list because they opposed the current regime or had simply angered someone in power. Denouncing a Tutsi, or even a Hutu with moderate political views, as being a "traitor" to Rwanda would become a common practice.

MASSACRE IN KIBUYE

Anti-Tutsi sentiment erupted in 1992, when a horrific massacre took place in the city of Kibuye, Rwanda. Tutsis were also killed in the area south

The Interahamwe

Habyarimana's party, the MRND, had an organization for young people called the Interahamwe, which loosely translates into "those who strike as one." The Interahamwe would soon become one of the most violent factions in the nation. Its thirty thousand young, mostly poor members were fed a steady diet of anti-Tutsi propaganda and false promises. The Interahamwe promised new recruits that they would get money, food, and perhaps even the homes and land of Tutsis they killed. As a result, they became Hutu extremists. They wore brightly colored red, green, and black shirts—the same colors as the Rwandan flag. Soon, they began carrying weapons such as machetes and wooden clubs. They also began compiling the names and addresses of Tutsis.

of Kigali and in the city of Gisenye, which is on the border that Rwanda shares with the Democratic Republic of the Congo (which was then known as Zaire). The killings were triggered by a fictitious report from the government claiming that the RPF was planning to kill a large number of Hutus. There was absolutely no element of truth to this report—the whole thing had been made up simply to provoke violence against Tutsis. Moderate Hutus, many of whom were political enemies of the regime, were also targeted. Hundreds of innocent people were killed.

ANOTHER OUTBREAK OF VIOLENCE

Tensions were ratcheted up again on October 21, 1993. In the neighboring country of Burundi, the democratically elected president, Melchior Ndadye, was assassinated. Ndadye, a Hutu, was killed by RPF soldiers. The RPF tried to assert control over Burundi, but it was driven back by Hutu forces. This failed coup ended with the deaths of thousands

The president of Burundi, Melchior Ndadye, was killed by RPF soldiers in 1993.

of Burundi Tutsis at the hands of Burundi Hutus. In retaliation, Tutsis killed Hutus.

Like Rwanda, Burundi had a population made up of Hutu, Tutsi, and a small number of Twa. Approximately three hundred thousand people, mostly Hutu, fled Burundi after Ndadye's death. They came to Rwanda as refugees. Hutu organizers entered the refugee camps and recruited heavily from among the Hutu refugees living there.

THE ARUSHA ACCORDS

After the killings, the Habyarimana government and the RPF declared a truce. They agreed to end the violence and the killings and signed a formal peace agreement on August 3, 1993. This agreement was known as the Arusha Accords, named for the city of Arusha, Tanzania, where it was signed.

The Arusha Accords were intended to end the violence against the Tutsis and halt the anti-Hutu RPF attacks. The accords stripped Habyarimana of much of his power, transferring it to an interim Rwandan government. This government would now allow members of the RPF to participate and engage in debates. RPF troops were supposed to be integrated into the FAR. The accords also guaranteed Rwandan exiles the right to return to their country.

There was chaos and killing after President Melchior Ndadye's death. Many Hutus fled Burundi and made their way to Rwanda.

Not everyone was a fan of the Arusha Accords, especially Habyarimana himself. Having held power in Rwanda for about twenty years, he was not anxious to relinquish it. Even though he lost a lot of his direct power over state affairs, Habyarimana retained the fanatical support of Hutu hard-liners.

Those responsible for the killing of Tutsis, however, were never brought to justice. The government had no intention of punishing anti-Tutsi murderers. Hutu groups like the Interahamwe quickly realized that there would be no legal repercussions for any crimes they might commit against Tutsis.

A FRAGILE PEACE

The United Nations sent a small peacekeeping force to Rwanda, under the leadership of Jacques-Roger Booh Booh from Cameroon. The mission's force commander was General Roméo Dallaire from Canada. The mission was entitled the United Nations Mission in Rwanda (UNAMIR) and was initially comprised of more than two thousand troops. The UN troops were primarily there to enforce the conditions of the Arusha Accords and to act as a deterrent to violence by reminding the nation's leaders that all the world was watching what happened in Rwanda.

But on November 18, 1993, only a few months after the Arusha Accords had been signed, violence broke out again. This time, twenty-one people were killed, and the murders were blamed on the RPF. However, UN observers were not so sure and reserved judgment. Hutu extremists took this to mean that the UN supported the Tutsis.

The relentless propaganda of the Hutu Power extremists, which was not only published in newspapers but also broadcast continually on their own radio station, Radio Télévision Libre des Mille Collins (RTLM), had succeeded in completely dividing the country. They relentlessly spread hatred against Tutsis, calling them *inyenze*, or cockroaches. There was no longer any room for political moderates or middle ground of any sort. Anyone who wavered in his or her support for the Habyarimana regime was branded a traitor.

THE GENOCIDE BEGINS

On April 6, 1994, the plane President Juvénal Habyarimana was traveling in was shot down, and he was killed. The Hutu president of Burundi, Cyprien Ntaryamira, also died in the crash. To this day, no one knows who is responsible for shooting down the plane. Some think that it was the RPF, while others believe it was Hutu extremists who were upset that Habyarimana had signed the Arusha Accords.

This RPF soldier examines the wreckage of Habyarimana's plane. To this day, no one knows who killed the Rwandan president. Some believe the RPF was responsible, while others think Habyarimana was killed by Hutu extremists who were dissatisfied with his policies.

The RPF denied that it had anything to do with Habyarimana's death, but it was blamed for it all the same. As soon as the news got out, ethnic violence exploded all over Rwanda. A concentrated campaign of killing, which lasted approximately one hundred days, would change the country forever.

3

The Genocide

Rwanda's genocide lasted only one hundred days. During this time, between eight hundred thousand and one million people were killed. The killings did not happen in secret—the United Nations, and the governments of the world, were briefed on what was happening. No one wanted to intervene. During these mass killings, the world looked on, and did nothing.

EARLY WARNINGS

On January 11, 1994, months before Habyarimana was killed, General Roméo Dallaire sent a fax to UN headquarters in New York City. The fax outlined information provided to UNAMIR from a Hutu informant who was in charge of training Interahamwe militia members. Although he could be killed if anyone found out he was talking to the UN, the informant refused to stand by while innocent civilians were killed.

The fax contained a startling amount of information about the violence that was about to engulf the country. The informant had told General Dallaire that Hutu extremists were planning to provoke the RPF into attacking them, in the hopes of breaking the Arusha Accords and creating a civil war.

Hutu Power extremists were also hoping to provoke the Belgian soldiers who were part of the UNAMIR force. Their plan was to get the Belgian soldiers to be the first to use a display of force. Then, Hutu hard-liners would counterattack and kill several Belgian soldiers. If this sequence of events unfolded, the Hutu extremists were convinced that Belgium would withdraw its troops from Rwanda. The Belgians were among the best-trained, best-equipped soldiers on the UNAMIR force.

General Dallaire's fax also detailed testimony from the informant that directly linked the FAR, the Interahamwe, and the Gendarmerie. Two thousand members of the Interahamwe were being trained in fighting techniques by the FAR. The informant believed that the Interahamwe was registering every single Tutsi in the country in order to be able to quickly, efficiently, and systematically exterminate the entire Tutsi population. In addition, he identified the location where the extremists were keeping their weapons. Everything mentioned in the fax would come to pass in the months that followed.

In exchange for all of this information, General Dallaire's informant wanted protection for himself and his family. He knew that if his identity was discovered, he would be killed. Dallaire asked the UN for permission to raid the extremists' weapons cache and to provide the informant with protection.

The UN responded that these requests went beyond the parameters of the mission. The UNAMIR troops were allowed to use force only if they were attacked directly. As a result, over the one hundred days of the genocide, UN troops would stand idly by and be unable to stop the killing of Tutsis going on all around them.

HATRED UNLEASHED

The names and addresses of nearly every one of Rwanda's Tutsis had been recorded. After Habyarimana's death, Tutsis were methodically hunted down and killed. The names and addresses of Tutsis were also read out

Roméo Dallaire

General Roméo Dallaire was born in 1946 and raised in Montreal, Canada. Dallaire rose through the ranks of the Canadian army, eventually attaining the rank of brigadier-general. In 1993, the UN picked Dallaire to be the force commander of its peacekeeping mission in Rwanda.

Initially there to implement the Arusha Accords, Dallaire watched the genocide unfold in front of his eyes. His requests for more money and additional troops were ignored by the United Nations. During the early 1990s, UN peacekeeping disasters in Somalia and the former Yugoslavia made UN member nations hesitant to intervene for peacekeeping purposes.

Dallaire stayed in Rwanda with a woefully small force of dedicated peacekeepers, trying to help those that he could. At the very least, he could bear witness to the events of the genocide. In August 1994, the stress became too much for Dallaire, and he asked to be relieved of his command. In 2000, he retired from the Canadian army. In 2004, Dallaire returned to Rwanda to testify against Colonel Théoneste Bagosora, one of the architects of the genocide. Since the genocide, Dallaire has continued to be active in international politics.

General Roméo Dallaire speaks with Tutsi refugees in May 1994.

over RTLM radio. While the killers went from door to door, slaughtering innocent people, the Interahamwe set up a series of roadblocks all over Kigali. Those attempting to drive through the city would be stopped at a roadblock and forced to present their identification cards. If they were Tutsi, they would be killed, often after being horribly tortured first.

The first people targeted in the genocide were moderate Hutu and Tutsi politicians who had not already fled or been killed. Nearly every single one of these officials was dead by April 7, 1994, the day after Habyarimana's plane was shot down.

Also on April 7, Hutu extremists captured ten Belgian UNAMIR soldiers. RTLM had spread the rumor that the Belgians and the Tutsis were both complicit in the assassination of the president. The captured Belgians were executed. Playing directly into Hutu hands, Belgium prepared to withdraw its soldiers from the UNAMIR force.

Many members of the RPF had family living in Kigali or other Rwandan towns and cities. For many of them, it was too difficult to maintain a cease-fire while their relatives were being killed or were under imminent threat of being killed. Therefore, the RPF attacked, violating the terms of the cease-fire that had already been ruptured by Hutu extremists and the army and police forces. The FAR responded in kind, and civil war erupted in Rwanda.

EVACUATION

By April 9, 1994, foreign nationals in Rwanda were being evacuated from the country. France and Belgium sent military forces to transport their citizens to safety. By April 12, everyone had been evacuated, and the Belgians had withdrawn from UNAMIR. By April 15, it became clear that the UN would not send any additional troops to halt the growing genocide.

The remaining UNAMIR force was very weak. It did not have enough soldiers or weapons to stop the killing by force even if the UN had

French soldiers evacuate European nationals from Rwanda on April 11, 1994. The majority of foreign troops would leave Rwanda shortly afterward. This would ultimately allow the genocide to occur unchecked.

allowed it to do so by expanding the parameters of its mission. According to General Agustin Bizimungu (a colonel in the FAR who was promoted to general the day after Habyarimana was killed), the genocide was being committed by rebel factions beyond his control. But with no leader in Rwanda exerting himself to check the power of the Hutu extremists, the FAR, Interahamwe, and Gendarmerie no longer attempted to conceal the fact that they were all working together in their efforts to exterminate the Tutsi population.

VOLUNTARY AND FORCED PARTICIPATION

Before the genocide began, not every Hutu in Rwanda was an extremist. The FAR, Gendarmerie, Interahamwe, and other militia groups made up a relatively small percentage of the Hutu population. But by the end of the genocide, a large percentage of the Hutu population had participated in the killings.

This participation could have been as simple as reporting that one's neighbors were Tutsi or as extreme as helping staff a roadblock where Tutsis were detained and killed. RTLM ceaselessly urged all Hutus to take up arms against the Tutsis, who were called traitors and cockroaches. The killers were men, women, and even children from all walks of life.

The majority of killers in Rwanda were normal civilians who took up arms against their countrymen. The killers didn't spare anyone—even children and pregnant women were targeted in the genocide. These genocidaires stand outside of a UN compound on April 13, 1994, waiting to get at the Tutsis inside.

Most of the killing was done with clubs and machetes, and Tutsi victims were generally tortured and mutilated. Women were often raped before being killed. No one was spared during the slaughter, not even children or pregnant women.

Not every Hutu was willing to kill. But those who refused to kill were often branded as traitors, a crime punishable by execution. Some Hutus who showed reluctance to take part in the genocide were forced to kill their neighbors. In such cases, a member of an extremist faction, such as the Interahamwe, would give them a club or a machete and tell them to kill. If they hesitated, or refused, they themselves would be killed on the spot.

These Tutsis flee into exile on May 25, 1994. Those Tutsis who were able to escape the genocide did. Many, however, were not so lucky.

Avoiding the slaughter was often a matter of luck more than anything else. Some Tutsis managed to maneuver past the roadblocks and roving bands of killers and escape to safety. Others managed to somehow hide themselves until the violence had ended. There were also a few very brave Hutus who used their authority, influence, or wits to help those Tutsis that they could. But the Rwandan genocide was a well-organized atrocity, and it was nearly impossible to escape it.

ORGANIZED MURDER

The genocide was organized on each and every level of Rwandan society. Organizers included politicians, members of the military, and business-people. The genocide would never have occurred if these people hadn't meticulously planned and directed it.

Colonel Théoneste Bagosora, the former leader of Habyarimana's Presidential Guard, was instrumental in provoking the genocide. He was close to Agathe Habyarimana, the widow of the former president. Agathe

Habyarimana was herself part of the Hutu extremist movement's inner circle, known as the *akuza* (which means "little house").

Prior to President Habyarimana's death, Bagosora was instrumental in the creation of the Interahamwe. He helped train them, transforming the

Colonel Théoneste Bagosora defends himself at a UN tribunal in Tanzania. Indicted for crimes against humanity, Bagosora is accused of masterminding the deaths of countless Rwandans.

young soldiers into a lethal fighting force. He also directed these young people in intelligence activities such as gathering information on Tutsis. Bagosora realized that there were not enough weapons in Rwanda to conduct a genocide, so he ordered that more weapons be imported.

The Rwandan government broadcast propaganda on RTML radio that encouraged people to take part in the violence. But in some areas in southern Rwanda, Hutus and Tutsis lived together in peaceful, fully integrated communities. In the early days of the conflict, many Hutus banded together with their Tutsi neighbors and friends. Interahamwe militias were instrumental in spreading the violence in the south, forcing Hutus to participate in the killing of their Tutsi friends and neighbors.

The existence of the Interahamwe also allowed those in power to distance themselves from the mass killings. Despite the fact that the army trained and directed the Interahamwe and other groups, they remained separate entities. When confronted by the UN, Hutu authorities could claim that the Interahamwe was composed of extremist factions that were acting independently.

The police force of Rwanda did nothing to stop the genocide. In fact, the police went door to door with members of the Interahamwe or FAR soldiers, slaughtering Tutsis. Early in the killing, Tutsis trying to save their lives begged the Gendarmerie to save them. Instead of protecting all Rwandans, which was their duty, the Gendarmerie killed Tutsis or brought in others to kill them.

Traditionally, churches have been places where people in trouble can go to seek sanctuary and escape harm. In Rwanda, this was not the case. The first episode of genocide witnessed by UNAMIR was at Gikondo Parish Church. On April 9, the Gendarmerie rounded up hundreds of Tutsi men, women, and children and brought them to the church. They then collected everyone's identification cards. The Gendarmerie invited militiamen into the church, and these soldiers killed every single Tutsi inside.

When it became clear that foreign governments would not intervene in the genocide, the killers felt no need to try and conceal their murders. Nearly the entire government, as well as the army and police, were complicit in what went on.

After the massacre, the identification cards of those killed were burned by the Gendarmerie. They also destroyed the official records of each person killed in an attempt to erase these individuals from existence.

THE APPEARANCE OF NORMALITY

The government tried to maintain the appearance of normal life during the genocide. People still went to work, and children still went to school. The government, police, and militias were all complicit in the genocide, and there were no media outlets criticizing what was going on. RTLM often used coded language when promoting the genocide, such as telling listeners to "crush cockroaches." Announcers often referred to the killing as "work," and reminded listeners to have their "tools" at hand.

Now, when Hutus gathered to take part in their obligatory work detail, such as building roads or clearing brush, they were instead expected to seek out and kill Tutsis. Religious leaders called community meetings, but the topic of conversation would not be love, peace, or brotherhood. Instead, it was extreme anti-Tutsi propaganda. Businesspeople did their part by donating money to the army, which was collecting for a "self-defense fund." The nature of this fund was not clearly defined, but the donated money went directly to the soldiers participating in the killing.

The efficiency of the killing during the Rwandan genocide is unparalleled in modern history. Never have so many people been killed so quickly. Prisoners were sent out to pick up the corpses filling the streets, homes, churches, and schools in Rwanda and load them into garbage trucks. Dogs roamed the streets of Kigali, feasting on the bodies of the dead.

RETRIBUTION

Meanwhile, the RPF, under the leadership of Rwanda's future president, Paul Kagame, made slow but steady progress against the FAR forces. Although they were outnumbered, members of the RPF benefited greatly from their superior training, discipline, and leadership. They captured more and more territory until, in July 1994, they occupied Kigali.

The city they took over was devastated. There were dead bodies everywhere, and buildings had been extensively looted. The sewage system was destroyed, and vandals had tainted the drinking water. There was no fuel, electricity, or phone service. And since the crops had gone unharvested for months, food was scarce.

The genocide had come to an end, but the violence did not stop right away. Now that the RPF controlled Kigali, a series of retribution murders against Hutus took place. About two million Hutus fled the

The RPF, led by Paul Kagame, was an extremely disciplined fighting force. Even though they were outnumbered, the RPF's superior training and ability were more than a match for their opponents.

country. The great majority ended up in Zaire (today known as the Democratic Republic of the Congo). It is believed that many of those who left had a hand in the killings. Living off of international aid in large refugee camps, they regrouped and kept their organization largely intact.

4

Survival

No one in Rwanda was untouched by the events that occurred in 1994. Ten percent of the population was killed, and only 25 percent of Tutsis living in Rwanda during the genocide survived. Nearly everyone knew someone who had been a killer or who had been killed. Almost every Rwandan, young and old, watched someone they knew get killed. Every Rwandan who lived through the genocide has a story to tell.

NYARUBUYE CHURCH

Nyarubuye Roman Catholic Church was the site of one of Rwanda's worst massacres. It is located in the province of Kibungo, sixty miles (ninety-six kilometers) east of Kigali. After Habyarimana was killed, Tutsis fled to the church, seeking sanctuary. The mayor of the town was a Hutu man named Sylvestre Gacumbitsi. He was the one who had told the Tutsis that they would be safe in the church. Less than ten days after Habyarimana was killed, Gacumbitsi led the police, as well as thousands of armed Hutus, to the church.

The killers told the Tutsis that they could buy their freedom. But after they handed over their money, they were killed anyway.

Boutros Boutros-Gali, the UN secretary general at the time of the genocide, is led through the human remains surrounding Nyarubuye Roman Catholic Church in 1995.

Grenades were tossed at the Tutsis hiding in the church, and they were shot at. Then the killers moved in with clubs and machetes, killing anyone who still survived inside. The bodies piled up, and blood was everywhere. Those inside begged for their lives or tried to fight back. However, they had no weapons. If they tried to escape, they were killed. The killing took so long that the killers had to work in shifts. Many of the killers slept outside the church at night, only to resume killing the next day. It took them four days before they were finished.

There were thousands of Tutsis hiding in the church. Those who survived managed to hide themselves among the bodies of the dead.

One of these survivors, a woman named Flora Mukampore, pretended to be dead. The killers found her and hit her in the head with a hammer, but still she lived. Mukampore hid among the bodies for an entire month, even after they had begun to badly decay. A thirteen-year-old girl named Valentina also survived by hiding among the bodies. She had been struck on the head and hand with a machete, but it did not kill her. Like Flora, she hid in the church, not coming out for forty-three days.

Many of those who survived the genocide were horrifically injured. This young girl, seen here on May 5, 1994, has sustained a head wound.

It was incredible that Flora and Valentina managed to survive such extreme brutality against such grim odds. Like all survivors, however, their lives would be changed forever. Valentina's family had been killed, and Flora lost seventeen family members. The Nyarubuye Church is now a monument to those who were killed.

HIDING IN THE HÔTEL DES MILLE COLLINES

Paul Rusesabagina was a Rwandan hotel manager who managed to save more than a thousand people from being killed during the genocide. Rusesabagina was a Hutu of mixed parentage (his father was a Hutu, his mother was a Tutsi). His wife, Odette Rusesabagina, was a Tutsi, and they had four children.

Rusesabagina was employed by Sabena Hotels, a Belgian company that had hotels in Kigali. Beginning in 1984, he worked for Sabena at the Hôtel des Mille Collines, eventually becoming its manager.

Rusesabagina would remain the manager of the Hôtel des Mille Collines until July 1994. During this time, he would use every resource at his disposal to protect himself, his family, and every single person who came to the hotel seeking refuge from the horrors occurring outside.

Rusesabagina had a number of resources at his fingertips that were not available to the average Rwandan. Some prominent extremists had Tutsi relatives or wives. They left them at the hotel during the genocide, believing this to be the safest place for them. It was therefore in their best interest that the hotel not be attacked. Rusesabagina bribed people with the money held in a safe in the Hôtel des Mille Collines. The hotel had a large stock of alcohol, which he also used to bribe people. Most of these bribes were simple—in one way or another, Rusesabagina convinced the killers to leave the hotel in peace. And as it filled up, more and more lives were on the line.

The Hôtel des Mille Collines was known to everyone in Kigali. Even though Rusesabagina was

Paul Rusesabagina, the hotel manager who saved thousands of lives during the genocide, speaks at the White House on February 17, 2005.

harboring Tutsis, important Hutus involved in the genocide would visit the hotel for drinks or to collect bribes. The fate of the hotel was completely at their mercy.

The people being sheltered in the hotel remained there for months. After the water supply was cut off, they used the water in the hotel's swimming pool. Rusesabagina had a lot of business contacts from his years working in the hotel business, and he took full advantage of them during the genocide. Rusesabagina arranged to procure alcohol to replace the hotel's stocks, depleted by all the bribes offered to Hutu soldiers. He also arranged for food to be delivered to sustain the hotel's growing number of refugees.

The hotel also had a special phone line that was used for its fax machine. Since it was separate from the hotel's other phone lines, it remained unaffected when they were cut. With this one phone line, Rusesabagina began making calls and sending faxes to anyone he thought might be able to help.

A very small UNAMIR force had been stationed outside the hotel, but it was not strong enough to repel a large-scale attack. On May 3, UNAMIR attempted to evacuate some of the refugees, including Rusesabagina's wife. There were sixty-two refugees in all, headed for the airport. They were offered asylum by the Belgian government. However, the evacuation did not go unnoticed. News of the convoy was brought to RTLM. The radio station immediately broadcast a warning to all listeners that there was a convoy of Tutsis trying to escape. With bloodthirsty mobs blocking their way, the convoy was forced to return to the hotel.

The RPF was steadily capturing more territory. If the people in the Hôtel des Mille Collines could find a way into RPF-controlled territory, they would be safe. On June 18, 1994, they did just that. UNAMIR escorted Rusesabagina and his family, along with all of the people they'd worked so hard to protect, to safety. The Rusesabagina family now lives in Belgium, where Paul owns a trucking company.

Refugees from the Hôtel des Mille Collines are evacuated by the UN on May 25, 1994. The 2004 film *Hotel Rwanda* was based on Paul Rusesabagina's efforts to help those who sought refuge inside the hotel.

STRANDED

Not everyone was lucky enough to find their way to the Hôtel des Mille Collines. For those Tutsis stranded among roving bands of drunken, machete-wielding Interahamwe members, staying alive was often just a matter of luck.

Eleven-year-old Hamis Kamuhanda watched members of the Interahamwe break into his house and drag his father off into the night. They fired indiscriminately into the Kamuhanda house, and Hamis pretended to be dead. To make sure he wasn't faking, one of the killers cut off his leg with a machete.

Hamis survived the attack. His mother and siblings did, too. Besides Hamis, none of them were gravely wounded. They could not risk trying to head for a hospital, and instead hid in the house until the RPF came. Had the RPF not managed to seize control of Kigali, and eventually, the entire country, it's possible that every last Tutsi left in Rwanda would have been killed.

5

Aftermath

After the genocide, Rwanda was left with the seemingly impossible task of rebuilding its economy, its infrastructure, its government, and its society. How could Hutus and Tutsis ever live together after what happened? It was clear that the future of Rwanda lay not in violence, but in peace.

JUSTICE

An entirely new government needed to be established in Rwanda. This new government was multiethnic, consisting of both Tutsis and Hutus. The new president of the country, Pasteur Bizimungu, was a Hutu, as were the prime minister and the majority of the government's cabinet members. Paul Kagame, a Tutsi and former leader of the RPF, became vice president and defense minister. He was elected president in 2003.

Approximately two million Hutus fled Rwanda after the RPF took control of the country. They lived in large refugee camps outside of Rwanda's borders. Hutu Power exiles regrouped there, recruiting new members and preparing to return to Rwanda when they were strong enough. Kagame launched an attack on the

Many Hutus fled Rwanda after the RPF took control of the country. The Hutus shown here, like many before them, are crossing into Tanzania. Before they were allowed into the country, however, they were forced to leave their machetes behind.

Democratic Republic of the Congo, where the largest refugee camps were, in order to force the refugees to return to Rwanda. There, they would be beholden to Rwandan law and would be imprisoned or reintegrated into society. Violence in the region sparked a new war that resulted in nearly four million deaths.

The new Rwandan government was faced with the problem of how to ensure that justice was served. The government estimates that about two million Hutus played a role in the genocide. It was clear that not every single killer could be caught and punished.

Instead, the government began arresting those who had a hand in organizing and promoting the genocide. They then went after the more notorious killers. Rwanda's prisons soon filled up with those who participated in the genocide. Prison overcrowding became a major problem: even if every Hutu who killed a Tutsi during the genocide was given a prison sentence, there would not be room for them all in Rwandan jails. Another problem was that safety could not always be guaranteed for those who testified against the killers. Many survivors of the genocide have been killed as a result of their testimony. As it stands, about five hundred people have been executed for their role in the genocide, and over one hundred thousand were imprisoned.

An RPF soldier guards Hutu prisoners. After the genocide, the new Rwandan government was faced with the difficult task of deciding how to punish the guilty.

Paul Kagame

Paul Kagame was born in southern Rwanda in 1957. His family went into exile in 1959, and he grew up as a refugee in Uganda. As a young man, Kagame gravitated toward military life. He formed the RPF in 1985. Kagame distinguished himself as a master tactician during the genocide. The superior discipline of the RPF troops allowed them to claim victory over the Hutu extremists. Kagame has been criticized for

not allowing dissenting political opinions to exist in Rwanda or allowing true freedom of the press. According to Kagame, this is to prevent his opponents from spreading divisive racial rhetoric.

Paul Kagame on July 20, 1994

Punishing the killers was only one obstacle for post-genocide Rwanda to overcome. A more pressing challenge was learning to live together as a nation once again. Hutus and Tutsis had lived side by side in the same neighborhoods before the genocide, and they did so again afterwards. Even if forgiveness might not have been possible right away, people had to learn to at least get along. There has been a concerted effort to bring people together, but violence and division have not yet been eliminated from Rwanda.

THE HUMAN COST

Tutsis were not the only victims of the genocide. Many Hutus were killed as well. Some of them were killed for political reasons, and most of these killings happened early on in the genocide. But others were killed for a great number of reasons. Some were accused of being Tutsis simply because they looked like Tutsis. Others were killed by personal enemies. So many people were being killed during the hundred days of the genocide that it was easy to literally get away with murder.

Those who survived the genocide still have many difficulties to overcome. Many people were mutilated during the genocide and have had to learn to live with their handicaps. Many others suffer from psychological problems such as post-traumatic stress disorder. The genocide also deprived many children of their parents, and there are thousands upon thousands of orphans in Rwanda today.

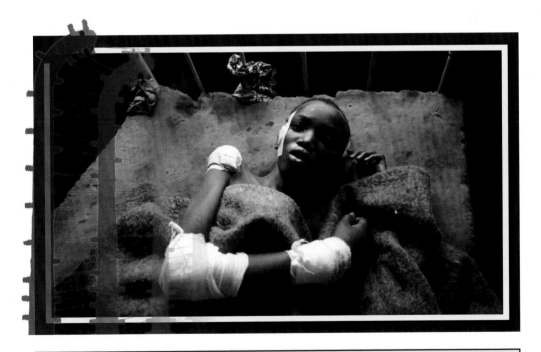

By the end of the genocide, Rwanda had many wounded people that needed medical attention. Organizations like Medecins Sans Frontieres worked to keep the hospitals open during the genocide.

It is believed that anywhere between 250,000 and 500,000 women were raped during the genocide. Most of the women who were raped were also killed. Life has not been easy for the survivors. Approximately 70 percent of these rape victims contracted the HIV virus, which was prevalent in Rwanda. Rwanda is an impoverished country, and it's rare that those with HIV can afford the expensive drug treatments that would keep them healthy and alive. Many female victims had children fathered by the rapists, which they then had to raise alone. They also had to live with the social stigma that their status as rape victims conferred upon them, and many were essentially ostracized by their communities.

NEVER AGAIN

Perhaps no one person can be directly blamed for the genocide. But many different people and groups share some of the responsibility for it. There are the killers and the organizations that helped them operate, like the Interahamwe. There are the businessmen who imported weapons such as machetes, knowing full well what they would be used for. There are the government leaders who led the killers to the Tutsis in their communities. There are the people who encouraged violence, like the staff of RTLM radio, and those in the Hutu extremist movement.

The responsibility even extends beyond the borders of Rwanda, encompassing a number of international entities that either supported the killers or refused to stop the violence. For instance, the weapons used to kill Tutsis were supplied to the Habyarimana regime by the French.

In this age of instantaneous communication and media saturation, it is impossible for foreign powers to claim that they were not informed about the Rwandan genocide. What happened in Rwanda happened in full view of the entire world. The simple fact is that no one wanted to get involved. Had the relatively small force General Dallaire asked for been granted to him, it would have sent a message to the extremists

There are many genocide memorials in Rwanda. This memorial is located in Nyamasheke, a province in western Rwanda.

that the world would not tolerate a ruthless mass murder. Instead, the international community ignored what was happening or refused to admit that it was actually a genocide. Once they admitted a genocide was occurring, they would have been bound by the UN to help stop it, and they did not want to contribute the money or troops to do so.

The killers knew that while powerful Western nations might claim to be committed to ending genocide, they would not involve themselves in a part of the world in which they had no political or economic stake. It seems that, in Rwanda, the only thing at stake was human life. Apparently, that wasn't enough.

Healing and reconciliation is a long process for Rwanda. On April 7, 2004, at a memorial service in Kigali marking the tenth anniversary of the genocide, President Paul Kagame lights a ceremonial flame for those Rwandans who were killed in the violence.

TEN YEARS LATER

A decade after the genocide, there are monuments all over the country to those who were killed. Former U.S. president Bill Clinton has apologized for his reluctance to use U.S. force to intervene in the genocide.

Kofi Annan, the head of UN Peacekeeping Operations during the genocide, has also accepted his share of responsibility for failing to prevent the genocide.

At a 2004 service marking the ten-year anniversary of the genocide, President Kagame made a speech about the events of a decade before. Addressing a capacity crowd in a Kigali stadium, he told them, "We cannot turn the clock back nor can we undo the harm caused, but we have the power to determine the future and to ensure that what happened never happens again."

There is still ethnic tension in Rwanda. While it may be some time until Rwanda's situation is stabilized, its economy is strengthening. Kagame is working to make Rwanda self-sufficient and to reduce its dependence on foreign aid. With any luck, Rwanda will have a bright future, and reconciliation will replace hatred and violence. And hopefully, the world has learned that it can no longer afford to watch the horrors of genocide unfold without trying to stop the killing of innocents.

TIMELINE

1918 Belgium assumes control of Rwanda. Tutsis are used to control the population of Rwanda and are shown favoritism in areas of employment and education.

1959–1962 During these tumultuous years, there is a Hutu uprising against the Tutsi and the Belgian colonists. Hutus win a great number of government elections. Thousands of Tutsis flee the country, fearing for their lives.

1963 A force comprised of Tutsi exiles sweeps into Rwanda, launching an attack on their home country. Hutus carry out reprisal killings against Tutsis living in Rwanda. These killings would continue sporadically for the next ten years.

1986 The RPF is formed. It will eventually come under the command of Rwanda's future president, Paul Kagame.

1926 All Rwandans are issued ethnic identity cards labeling them as being Hutu, Tutsi, or Twa.

1962 Rwanda achieves its independence from Belgium. The Belgian colonists withdraw from the country.

1973 General Juvénal Habyarimana becomes president of Rwanda. Although discrimination against Tutsis persists, violence against them largely ceases before resuming in the early 1990s.

October 1990 An RPF force, numbering a few hundred, invades Rwanda. They are eventually repelled.

1992 The Kibuye Massacre occurs.

1993 The RPF launches attacks on Kigali.

August 3, 1993 The Arusha Peace Accords are signed in Arusha, Tanzania. The UN sends troops to ensure that they are carried out.

November 18, 1993 Violence breaks out as twenty-one innocent people are killed. Their deaths are blamed on the RPF, although there seems to be evidence to the contrary.

January 11, 1994 Roméo Dallaire sends a fax to UN headquarters, detailing how the Hutu extremist movement is stockpiling weapons and preparing to commit violent acts against UN soldiers and innocent Tutsis. The UN does not approve Dallaire's proposed plan of action in response to this information.

April 6, 1994 The plane carrying Rwandan president Juvénal Habyarimana and Cyprien Ntayamira, the president of Burundi, is shot down by unknown assailants.

April 7, 1994 The genocide begins.

April 8, 1994 UNAMIR soldiers see the first evidence of mass murder of Tutsis at the Gikondo Parish Church.

April 12, 1994 All foreign nationals are evacuated from Rwanda.

April 21, 1994 The UN withdraws the majority of its troops from Rwanda, leaving behind only a small force of a few hundred.

July 1994 The genocide against Tutsis is effectively brought to an end when the RPF captures the city of Kigali. Sporadic killings still occur throughout the country.

December 1996 Trials begin for those accused of participating in the genocide.

2003 Paul Kagame is elected president of Rwanda.

GLOSSARY

aristocracy A group of rich and powerful people, often born into their positions of privilege. In monarchies, aristocrats are given a large role in the functioning of a government.

colonialism The practice of a powerful country conquering a less powerful region, establishing political control over it, and exploiting it in order to extract wealth and resources.

ethnicity A distinctive group set apart from others by a common culture, language, or place of origin.

exhort To strongly urge or warn.

exterminate To kill every single member of a group of humans or animals.

genocide The organized and systematic attempt to completely destroy a group of people, through murder or other means.

hard-liner A person who adheres to a strict and sometimes extreme set of beliefs.

Hutu Power A movement based on the ideas that Hutus ought to support each other and oppose other ethnic groups. Hutu Power originated in the Rwandan social revolution of 1959.

implement To carry out a plan or program.

Interahamwe A militia group, made up of largely disaffected young Hutus, who were the foot soldiers of the genocide. Their name means "those who strike as one" or "those who stand together."

manual labor Work done with the hands, as opposed to other types of work.

Nazi A shortened name for the National Socialist Party, which ruled Germany during World War II. All other political parties were outlawed in Germany from 1933 to 1945. Led by Adolf Hitler, the Nazi Party established a racist, anti-Semitic, homophobic state that aimed to conquer as much of Europe as possible and to subjugate or exterminate races that it considered inferior.

peacekeeping Refers to military missions in which international troops are given a mission to prevent violence between two warring groups, keep the peace, or bolster law and order in war zones. It may also involve humanitarian work, human rights monitoring, and assistance in honoring the terms of a peace agreement.

propaganda Media created solely to influence people's views. Negative propaganda is often used to turn public sentiment against a group of people or political party.

recruit To find new members for a group, such as a political party or army.

Roma An ethnic group commonly referred to as gypsies. Communities of Roma can be found all over the world, although they are concentrated in Europe. A frequent target of discrimination, Roma were once a largely nomadic people.

subsistence agriculture Agriculture practiced by individual households, which usually provides just enough food to feed one family over the course of a year.

United Nations (UN) An organization created to promote peace, stability, economic cooperation, and security around the world. The United Nations aims to bring the nations of the world together to talk, to work together to solve common problems, and to resolve conflicts.

FOR MORE INFORMATION

American Red Cross National Headquarters
2025 E Street NW
Washington, DC 20006
(703) 206-6000
Web site: http://www.redcross.org
   Established in 1881, the Red Cross is an international humanitarian organization.

Amnesty International USA
5 Penn Plaza
New York, NY 10001
(212) 807-8400
Web site: http://www.amnestyusa.org
   Amnesty International works to safeguard human rights around the world. It is a nonprofit, nongovernmental institution.

Doctors Without Borders
333 7th Avenue, 2nd Floor
New York, NY 10001-5004
(212) 679-6800
Web site: http://www.doctorswithoutborders.org
   Doctors Without Borders is a nongovernmental organization that provides medical aid to countries that need it. The organization is active in nations facing widespread disease or that have suffered through war and violence.

Human Rights Watch
350 Fifth Avenue, 34th Floor
New York, NY 10118

(212) 290-4700
Web site: http://www.hrw.org
   Human Rights Watch works to safeguard human rights. It is a
   nongovernmental organization that extends its efforts internationally.

Oxfam America
226 Causeway Street, 5th Floor
Boston, MA 02114
(800) 776-9326
Web site: http://www.oxfamamerica.org
   Oxfam America is a part of Oxfam International, a nongovernmental
   organization that works to find solutions to human rights abuses,
   famine, poverty, and injustice.

United Nations Headquarters
First Avenue at 46th Street
New York, NY 10017
Web site: http://www.un.org
   The United Nations was founded in 1945. Headquartered in New York,
   the UN works to bring nations together to mediate international
   disputes and promote peace and stability.

WEB SITES

Due to the changing nature of Internet links, Rosen Publishing has
developed an online list of Web sites related to the subject of this book.
This site is updated regularly. Please use this link to access the list:

http://www.rosenlinks.com/gmt/gerw

FOR FURTHER READING

Bodnarchuk, Kari. *Rwanda: Country Torn Apart* (World in Conflict). Minneapolis, MN: Lerner Publishing Group, 1999.

Carr, Rosamund Halsey. *Land of a Thousand Hills: My Life in Rwanda*. New York, NY: Penguin Putnam, 2000.

King, David C. *Cultures of the World: Rwanda*. New York, NY: Benchmark Books, 2007.

Meredith, Martin. *The Fate of Africa: From the Hopes of Freedom to the Heart of Despair*. New York, NY: Public Affairs, 2005.

Mitchell, Peter, ed. *Peoples and Cultures of Africa: Central Africa*. New York, NY: Facts On File, 2006.

Murray, Jocelyn, and Brian A Stewart. *Africa* (Cultural Atlas for Young People). New York, NY: Chelsea House Publications, 2007.

Reader, John. *Africa*. Washington, DC: National Geographic Society, 2001.

Rusesabagina, Paul, and Tom Zoellner. *An Ordinary Man: An Autobiography*. New York, NY: Viking Penguin, 2006.

Shillington, Kevin. *History of Africa*. New York, NY: Palgrave Macmillan, 2005.

BIBLIOGRAPHY

Amanpour, Christiane. "Looking Back at Rwandan Genocide." CNN.com. April 6, 2004. Retrieved November 2007 (http://edition.cnn.com/2004/WORLD/africa/04/06/rwanda.amanpour/index.html).

BBC News. "Eyewitness: A Survivor's Story." April 2, 2001. Retrieved November 2007 (http://news.bbc.co.uk/2/hi/africa/1252049.stm).

BBC News. "UN Admits Rwanda Genocide Failure." April 15, 2000. Retrieved November 2007 (http://news.bbc.co.uk/1/hi/world/africa/714025.stm).

Dallaire, Roméo A., and Brent Beardsley. *Shake Hands with the Devil: The Failure of Humanity in Rwanda*. New York, NY: Carroll & Graf Publishers, 2004.

Fischer, Ian. "Hutu and Tutsi: Is a Unified Rwanda Possible?" *New York Times*, April 6, 1999. Retrieved November 2007 (http://query.nytimes.com/gst/fullpage.html?res=9A03E2DE1E39F935A35757C0A96F958260&sec=&spon=&pagewanted=1).

Goodman, Walter. "Young Witness to Rwanda Massacre." *New York Times*, April 1, 1997. Retrieved November 2007 (http://query.nytimes.com/gst/fullpage.html?res=9B07E7DD1E3AF932A35757C0A961958260).

Gourevitch, Philip. *We Wish to Inform You That Tomorrow We Will Be Killed with Our Families: Stories from Rwanda*. New York, NY: Picador USA, 1998.

Human Rights Watch. *Leave None to Tell the Story: Genocide in Rwanda*. March 1999. Retrieved November 2007 (http://www.hrw.org/reports/1999/rwanda/index.htm#TopOfPage).

Human Rights Watch. "Rwanda: Killings Threaten Justice For Genocide." January 22, 2007. Retrieved November 2007 (http://hrw.org/english/docs/2007/01/19/rwanda15126.htm).

Keane, Fergal. "Deliver Us from Evil." *Independent*, April 3, 2004. Retrieved November 2007 (http://findarticles.com/p/articles/mi_qn4158/ is_20040403/ai_n12785209).

Lacey, Marc. "10 Years Later in Rwanda, the Dead Are Ever Present." *New York Times*, February 26, 2004. Retrieved November 2007 (http://query.nytimes.com/gst/fullpage.html?res=9401E3DB133CF 935A15751C0A9629C8B63).

Lorch, Donatella. "Heart of Rwanda's Darkness: Slaughter at a Rural Church." *New York Times*, June 3, 1994. Retrieved November 2007 (http://query.nytimes.com/gst/fullpage.html?res=9A0DE0DE1E3BF 930A35755C0A962958260).

Prunier, Gérard. *The Rwanda Crisis: History of a Genocide*. New York, NY: Columbia University Press, 1995.

United Nations. "Statement on Receiving the Report of the Independent Inquiry into the Actions of the United Nations During the 1994 Genocide in Rwanda." December 16, 1999. Retrieved November 2007 (http://www.un.org/News/ossg/sgsm_rwanda.htm).

INDEX

ABOUT THE AUTHOR

Frank Spalding is a writer based in New York State. He has had a lifelong interest in politics and international affairs.

PHOTO CREDITS

Cover (top), pp. 4 (left), 7, 14, 24, 36, 43 Pascal Guyot/AFP/Getty Images; cover (bottom), p. 50 Str/AFP/Getty Images; pp. 4–5, 47 Paula Bronstein/ Getty Images; p. 8 © Geoatlas; p. 9 © Roger-Viollet/The Image Works; p. 10 Henry Guttmann/Hulton Archive/Getty Images; p. 12 © Hulton-Deutsch Collection/Corbis; p. 15 Keystone/Hulton Archive/Getty Images; pp. 16, 21, 23, 26, 28, 29, 30, 33, 35, 38, 41 Scott Peterson/Getty Images; pp. 18, 46 Alexander Joe/AFP/Getty Images; p. 20 Dabrowski/AFP/Getty Images; p. 31 Kennedy Ndahiro/AFP/Getty Images; p. 37 Corinne Dufka/ AFP/Getty Images; p. 39 Tim Sloan/AFP/Getty Images; p. 44 David C. Turnley/KRT Photo/Newscom; p. 45 Abdelhak Senna/AFP/ Getty Images; p. 49 Jose Cendon/AFP/Getty Images.

Designer: Tahara Anderson; Photo Researcher: Cindy Reiman